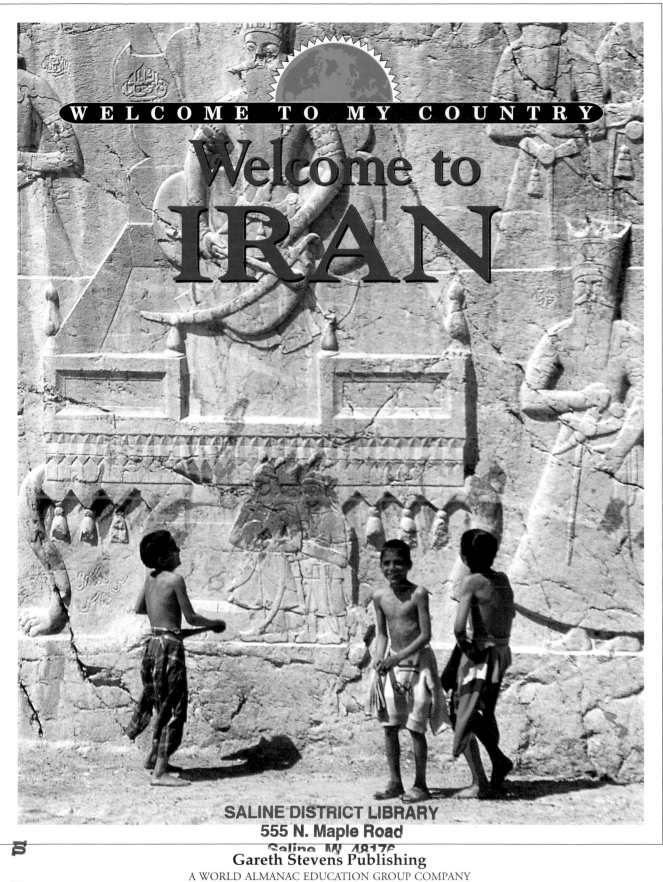

WELCOME TO MY COUNTRY

Welcome to
IRAN

Gareth Stevens Publishing
A WORLD ALMANAC EDUCATION GROUP COMPANY

Written by
DORA YIP/MARIA O'SHEA

Edited in USA by
DOROTHY L. GIBBS

Designed by
HASNAH MOHD ESA

Picture research by
SUSAN JANE MANUEL

First published in North America in 2001 by
Gareth Stevens Publishing
A World Almanac Education Group Company
330 West Olive Street, Suite 100
Milwaukee, Wisconsin 53212 USA

Please visit our web site at:
www.garethstevens.com
For a free color catalog describing
Gareth Stevens' list of high-quality books
and multimedia programs, call
1-800-542-2595 (USA) or
1-800-461-9120 (CANADA).
Gareth Stevens Publishing's
Fax: (414) 332-3567.

© **TIMES MEDIA PRIVATE LIMITED 2001**
Originated and designed by
Times Editions
An imprint of Times Media Private Limited
A member of the Times Publishing Group
Times Centre, 1 New Industrial Road
Singapore 536196
http://www.timesone.com.sg/te

Library of Congress Cataloging-in-Publication Data
Yip, Dora.
Welcome to Iran / Dora Yip and Maria O'Shea.
p. cm. — (Welcome to my country)
Includes bibliographical references and index.
ISBN 0-8368-2525-X (lib. bdg.)
1. Iran—Juvenile literature. [1. Iran.]
I. O'Shea, Maria. II. Title. III. Series.
DS254.75.Y57   2001
955—dc21   2001025019

Printed in Malaysia

1 2 3 4 5 6 7 8 9 05 04 03 02 01

PICTURE CREDITS
Archive Photos: 16
Focus Team: 45
HBL Network: 19, 34, 36, 37
The Hutchison Library: 2, 25
Earl Kowall: 1, 3 (bottom), 4, 6, 17, 26, 32, 41
Nazima Kowall: cover, 3 (center), 5, 20, 21,
    23, 24, 30, 33
North Wind Picture Archives: 11
Christine Osborne: 3 (top), 35
Maria O'Shea: 44 (both)
Topham Picturepoint: 14, 15 (bottom)
Trip Photographic Library: 7, 8, 9 (both), 10,
    15 (top), 18, 22, 27, 28, 29, 31, 38, 39, 40
Vision Photo Agency: 12, 13

Digital Scanning by Superskill Graphics Pte Ltd

Contents

Words that appear in the glossary are printed in **boldface** type the first time they occur in the text.

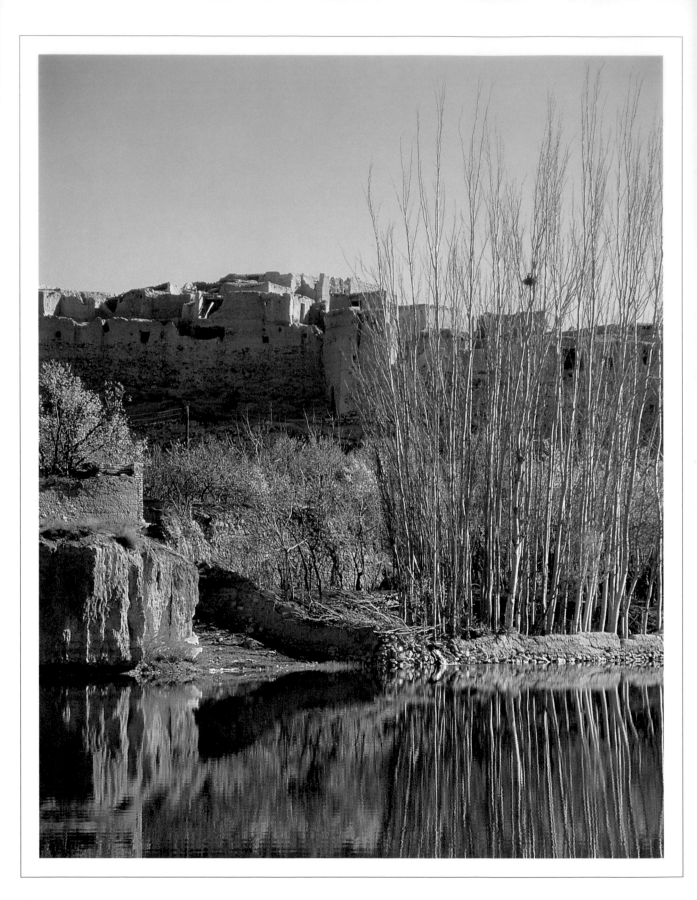

4

Welcome to Iran!

Present-day Iran was officially named the Islamic Republic of Iran in 1979. Although Iran is a young nation, its history dates back thousands of years. It was once the center of the powerful Persian Empire (559–330 B.C.). Let's visit Iran and learn about its history and its people!

Opposite: Some villages in Iran were built between the second and seventh centuries.

Below: Royal Square, in the city of Esfahan, is one of the largest town squares in the world.

The Flag of Iran

The Iranian flag has green, white, and red bands. Green represents the Islamic religion. White stands for peace. Red recognizes the courage and loyalty of Iran's people. The red **emblem** on the white band is Iran's national symbol.

The Land

With an area of 636,296 square miles (1,648,000 square kilometers), Iran is twice as big as Texas. Deserts cover much of the country's central and eastern areas.

Except along the coasts, Iran lies on a **plateau**. An **elevation** of 4,000 feet (1,219 meters) makes this country one of the highest in the world.

Below:
The snowcapped Zagros Mountains separate Iran from the country of Iraq.

6

Three mountain ranges cut across the Iranian plateau. The Markazi range stretches from northwest to southeast. The Zagros range is in the west and southwest. The Elburz Mountains in the north contain Iran's highest peak, Mount Damavand, at 18,606 feet (5,671 m). The Caspian Sea, which is the largest lake in the world, lies directly north of the Elburz Mountains.

Above:
Flamingos wade in Iran's coastal waters near the Persian Gulf.

7

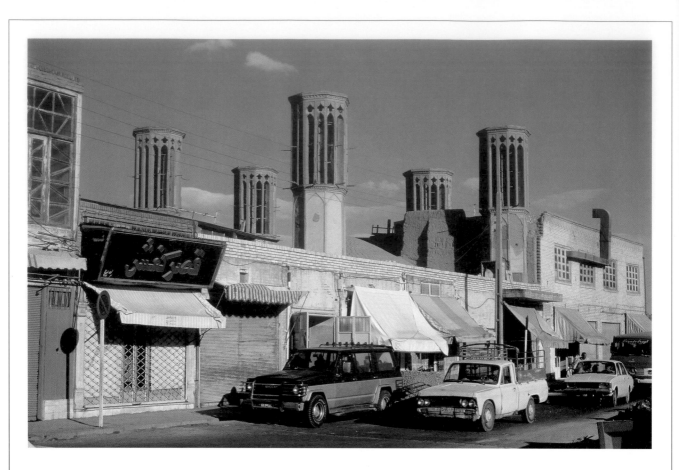

Climate

Northwestern and western Iran have four seasons, including a very cold winter. During winter, temperatures can be as low as -35° Fahrenheit (-37° Celsius). Southern and eastern Iran have only two seasons — a hot summer and a mild, rainy winter. The provinces along the Caspian Sea have a **subtropical** climate. The Elburz Mountains trap humidity in this area.

Above: Houses in the hottest parts of Iran are designed to stay cool inside. The tall towers on their rooftops have openings to catch outside breezes. This air flows down to the basement, where a pool or stream cools it. The cool air then **circulates** all through the house.

Plants and Animals

Due to its climate and high altitude, Iran does not have much plant life. Most of its forests are in the humid Caspian region, where oak, ash, elm, and beech trees grow. Smaller, shrub-like trees grow in some of the drier areas. Slender poplars are the most common trees in Iran.

Iran has many areas that are not suitable for people to live in, so wild animals have made homes in them. These animals include bears, lynxes, leopards, jackals, hyenas, and wolves.

Above: Iranian pomegranates are believed to be the reddest and tastiest in the world. People in Iran use every part of the pomegranate tree, either for food or to make dye or medicine.

Left: The deserts of Iran are home to many reptiles, including the rare pygmy gecko (*Tropiocolotes latifi*).

History

Archaeologists have found signs of human life in the Zagros Mountains dating back to 100,000 B.C. By about 6000 B.C., settlers and farmers lived throughout the Iranian plateau.

Around 2500 B.C., the Elamites living on the Khuzestan plains set up a **feudal** system of government that lasted until the sixth century B.C. By then, the Medes and the Parsua, or Persians, had taken over Iran.

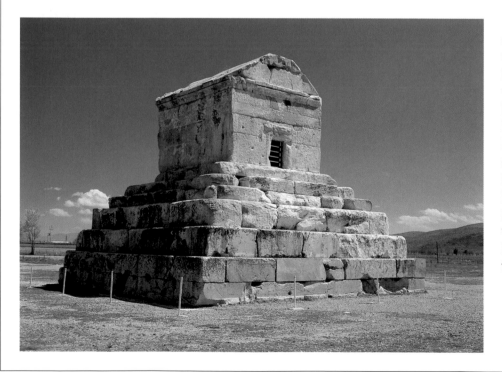

Left: The tomb of Persian king Cyrus the Great is in Pasargadae, which is located in southwestern Iran. Cyrus made Pasargadae the capital of the Persian Empire because it was near the place where his army had defeated the Medes.

The Persian Empire

In mid sixth-century B.C., the Persians, led by King Cyrus II, defeated the Medes and created a vast empire. At its peak, the Persian Empire included Egypt, Central Asia, northern India, and Ionian Greek lands.

The Persian Empire ended when Greek ruler Alexander the Great conquered Persepolis in 330 B.C. In A.D. 651, Persia fell to the Arabs, who ruled until the thirteenth century.

Above: In 479 B.C., the Greek (*right*) and Persian (*left*) armies fought the Battle of Plataea. Alexander the Great admired the skill and techniques of the Persian army so much that he trained Greek troops to fight the same way.

From Empires to Revolutions

Although Mongol invasions in the 1200s destroyed much of the Persian culture, Shah Abbas I of the Safavid **dynasty** was able to reunite Persia's kingdoms in the sixteenth century. Abbas's successors, however, could not stop the Ottoman Turks and other invaders from conquering many parts of the country. By 1900, Persia had been reduced to approximately the size it is today.

Above: Shah Abbas the Great ruled Persia from 1588 to 1629. He was a wise ruler, and, during his reign, the country regained some of its lost glory.

In 1921, a young army officer named Reza Khan took control of Iran's armed forces. In 1925, Reza Khan became Reza Shah Pahlavi, **sovereign** ruler of Iran. The reforms made during his rule were very unpopular, especially with Muslim religious leaders.

Reforms made by his successor, Muhammad Reza Shah Pahlavi, who was his son, were not widely accepted either. Some of Muhammad Reza

Shah Pahlavi's social and economic changes became known as the "White Revolution." These reforms included redistributing land and allowing women more freedom.

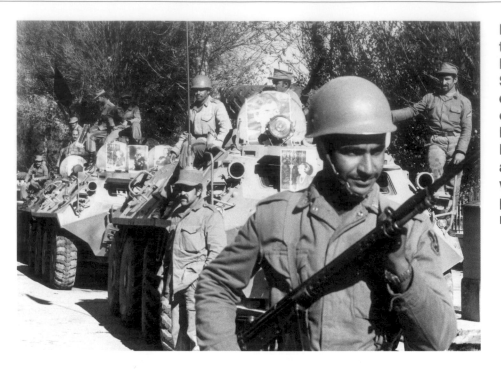

Left: In 1979, troops supporting Muhammad Reza Shah Pahlavi entered the city of Esfahan to stop Iranian rebels. Many of the troops' armored vehicles were covered with portraits of the royal family.

The 1978–1979 Revolution

Iranians revolted against the shah's government in 1978, and on April 1, 1979, rebel leader Ruhollah (Ayatollah) Khomeini established the Islamic Republic of Iran. Many Iranians who opposed Khomeini's government were **persecuted** or killed.

With Iran in a state of political unrest, neighboring Iraq tried to reclaim parts of southwestern Iran. The Iranians fought back, waging a war that lasted ten years and claimed a million lives. Iraq withdrew its troops in 1990.

Cyrus the Great (c. 590/580–529 B.C.)

While Cyrus II was king of Persia, he established an empire that stretched from Central Asia to Egypt. He was a strong and wise ruler.

Muhammad Reza Shah Pahlavi (1919–1980)

The son of Reza Shah Pahlavi, Muhammad Reza Shah Pahlavi became Iran's sovereign leader in 1941. His **autocratic** rule led to the 1978–1979 revolution, which forced him into **exile**.

Muhammad Reza Shah Pahlavi

Ruhollah Khomeini (c. 1900–1989)

Muslim scholar Ruhollah Khomeini was one of Iran's most influential religious leaders. He was against Muhammad Reza Shah Pahlavi and convinced Iranians to rebel. Under Khomeini's leadership, Iran followed strict Islamic laws.

Ruhollah Khomeini

Government and the Economy

Government and Administration

Iran is an Islamic country ruled by a supreme spiritual leader, or *faqih* (fah-KEEH). The faqih makes sure the country is governed according to Islamic laws. The current faqih is Ayatollah Ali Khamenei.

Above: Muhammad Khatami was elected president of Iran in 1997. He has worked to improve relations with the West.

Iran's president, who is elected to a four-year term, is the head of state. The president chooses a cabinet of twenty-four ministers. The *Majlis* (MAJ-liss), or the Islamic Consultative Assembly, passes laws and makes economic decisions. The Council of Guardians, which is a group of twelve Islamic judges and scholars, supervises elections and makes sure that all laws follow Islamic beliefs.

Each of Iran's twenty-eight provinces has a governor-general, and each city elects a mayor.

The Legal System

Iranian laws are based on the Qur'an, which is the holy book of Islam. Other instructions come from the Hadith, which contains teachings of the prophet Muhammad. Iran's legal system has levels of courts ranging from civil courts to a Supreme Court. Since Iranian courts follow Islamic laws, judges act without **juries**.

Below: The Elburz Mountains tower over the city of Tehran, which is the capital of Iran.

The Economy

Iran's economy has depended on oil, the country's most valuable resource, for many years. Recently, however, Iran's economy has suffered. First, the war with Iraq created huge debts. Then, U.S. **sanctions** damaged trading, and oil prices and investments in industry fell.

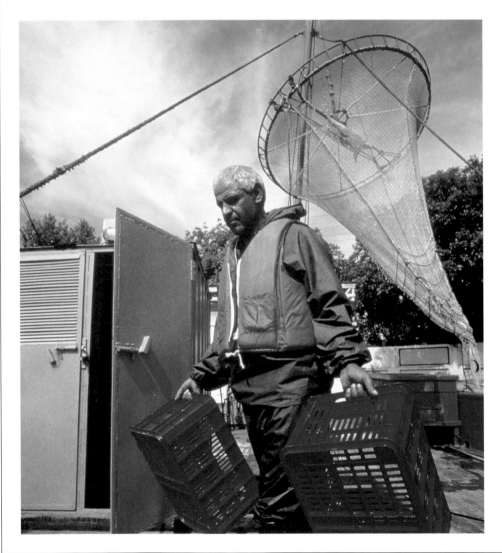

Left: Crates and fishing nets are some of the equipment loaded onto fishing boats to help bring in the day's catch. Fishing, forestry, and agriculture make important contributions to Iran's economy.

Industry and Agriculture

Besides oil refining, Iran's large industries include iron and copper mining and textile, automobile, and carpet manufacturing.

Although less than half of the land in Iran is suitable for crops, more than one-third of the population works in

Below: This Iranian worker is inspecting cans of food.

agriculture. Wheat and barley are the country's most important crops. Farmers also grow cotton, potatoes, rice, fruits, nuts, and sugar beets.

People and Lifestyle

Iran is home to many **ethnic** groups. Persians number only slightly more than half of the population. Other groups include the Azerbaijanis, Kurds, Arabs, Baluchis, Lurs, and Turkmen. **Nomadic** groups, such as the Qashqai and the Bakhtiari, have lived in Iran for centuries. The Iranian government, however, tries to discourage their wandering lifestyles.

Below: Many of today's Iranians can trace their roots back to the Aryan groups who came to Iran from Central Asia in the second century B.C.

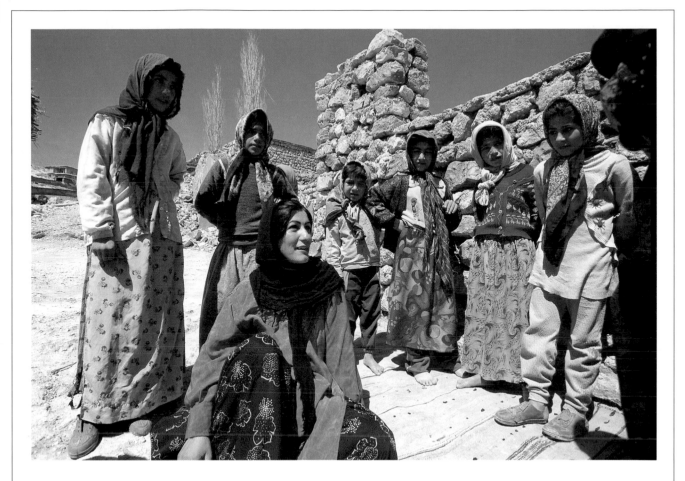

More and more people in Iran are moving from farms and villages to cities. The cities offer greater opportunities for employment and education, as well as better health care and living conditions. About 60 percent of Iranians now live in cities, and more than one-sixth of the total population lives in Iran's capital city, Tehran.

Above: The Lurs and other minority groups live close to Iran's borders. The government wants minorities to become part of Iranian society, but some groups, especially Kurds, have struggled for a long time to be independent.

Family Life

The family is at the center of Iranian life. Family members are very close. Due to changing lifestyles, Iranian families are smaller today than in the past, but households are still large. Several generations often live together. Even when young Iranians leave home, they like to live close to their parents. Very few people live alone in Iran, and almost everyone considers marriage important. Iranians see marriage as an opportunity to expand the family.

Marriage

Islamic law allows an Iranian man to have as many as four wives. Most, however, have only one. In a divorce, children stay with their father.

Below:
Older citizens are respected in Iranian society. Iranians believe that wisdom comes with age.

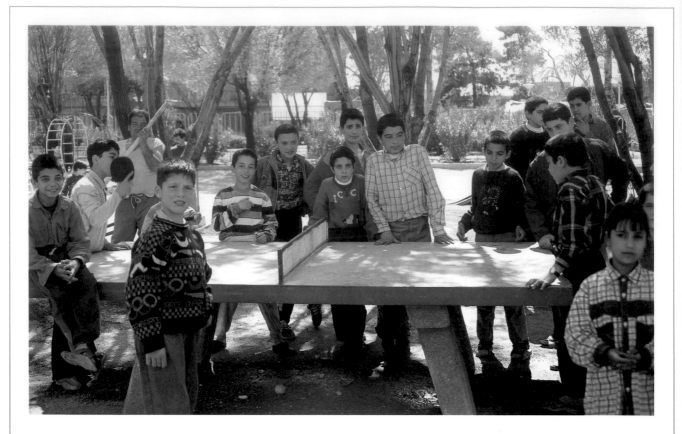

Education

Iranians value education and have high academic standards. All Iranian children must attend school between the ages of six and fourteen. Public education is free through high school.

Getting into an Iranian university is very difficult. Most students spend up to a year preparing for the entrance examinations. Nevertheless, more than a million Iranians currently attend institutions of higher learning. The universities in Tehran are generally considered the best.

Religious Education

Many children in Iran attend weekly Qur'an classes taught by a Muslim religious expert called a *mullah* (MOO-lah). Some young men go to religious schools that prepare them for **seminary** training to become a mullah.

Below: In most Iranian schools, girls and boys are taught separately. Boys are taught by men. Girls are taught by women.

Religion

Ninety-nine percent of Iran's people are Muslims. Muslims believe in one God, Allah, and that Muhammad, the founder of Islam, was Allah's last prophet. Eighty-nine percent of Iran's Muslims are Shi'ites. Ten percent are Sunnis. Shi'ite Muslims recognize only Muhammad's descendants as rightful leaders of the Islamic world. Sunni Muslims accept other leaders.

Below: The area outside a mosque, the place where Muslims worship, is very busy after Friday prayers. These women are leaving a mosque in the city of Esfahan.

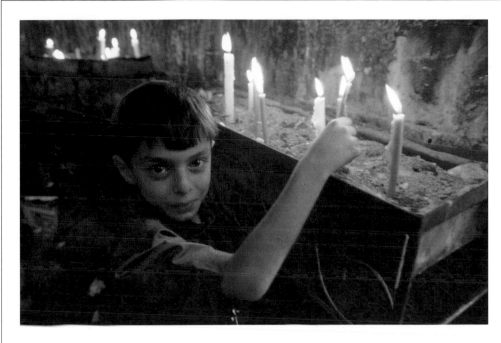

One percent of Iran's population is not Muslim. Non-Muslims are free to practice their own religions, as long as they respect Islam. Non-Muslim religious groups in Iran include Jews; Christians, who are mainly Orthodox Armenians; and **Zoroastrians**.

Iran's largest group of non-Muslims are followers of the Baha'i faith. The Iranian government, however, considers this religion anti-Islamic, or against Islam. Baha'is believe that all world religions share one message and the same God.

Language

The official language of the Islamic Republic of Iran is Persian, which is also called Farsi. Only about half of the Iranian people, however, speak Farsi as a first language. About one-fourth of the population speaks Turkic languages.

Farsi shares root words with most European languages, such as English, German, French, and Spanish. English words taken from the Farsi language include *khaki*, *pajamas*, and *paradise*.

Left: Iranians enjoy reading many types of books and newspapers.

Left: The tombs of thirteenth- and fourteenth-century poets Saadi and Hafez are in the city of Shiraz. Hafez's tomb is inside this small pavilion, which was built in 1953.

Literature

Poetry is Iran's most well-known form of literature. The most famous Iranian poet known outside the country is Omar Khayyam. His *Rubaiyat*, written in the eleventh century, has been translated into English and many other languages. Two other admired Iranian poets are Saadi and Hafez.

Iranian writers often use their work to examine Iranian life and educate the public. Many writers have been punished by the government for their negative views.

Arts

Iran's most widely known art form is handmade carpets. Throughout the world, Persian carpets are found in grand hotels, stately mansions, and ordinary homes. In Iran, every home has beautiful carpets.

The carpets from each region of the country have their own distinct colors and patterns. The rich colors

Below: Persian carpets are made of wool or silk that is tied by hand to a base of cotton or silk threads. High-quality carpets can have up to 93,000 knots per square foot (over 1 million knots per square meter). Experienced carpet makers can tie 10,000–14,000 knots a day.

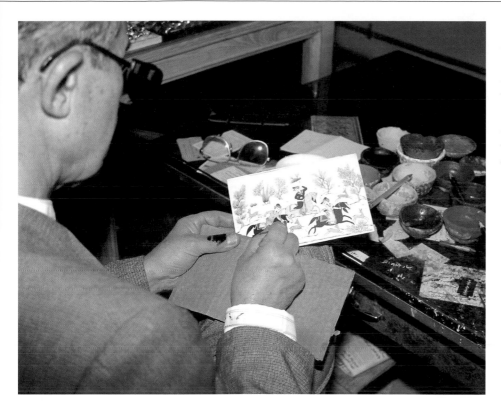

Left: Iranian artists are masters of the miniature painting art form. This tradition has been passed on from one generation to the next since the twelfth century.

come from plant dyes. Common patterns include flowers, fruits, and animals. The highest-quality carpets are made of silk.

Miniature Paintings

Using brushes that have a single hair, Iranian artists create paintings so tiny that details often cannot be seen without a magnifying glass. The images are usually painted onto bone or leather.

Crafts and Calligraphy

Metalsmiths, woodworkers, and jewelers are some of the Iranian artists who sell their handcrafted products in Iran's bazaars, or marketplaces.

Iranian artists also use calligraphy, which is the art of elegant handwriting and lettering, to decorate everything from carpets and wall tiles to banners

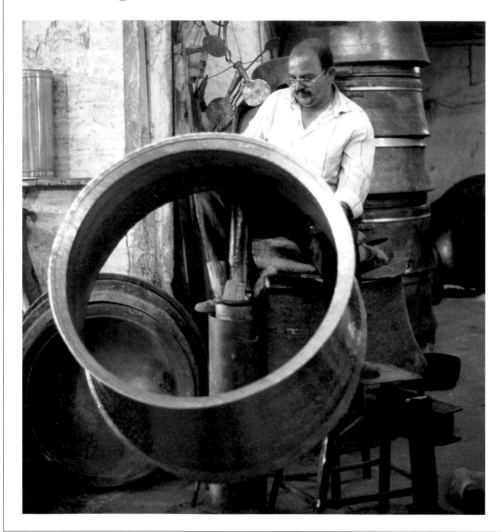

Left: Craftspeople in Iran, such as this coppersmith, spend a long time learning a trade before being considered skilled **artisans**.

and paintings. Calligraphy **inscriptions** are usually inspired by the writings in the Qur'an.

Architecture

Architecture is one of the most beautiful expressions of Iranian art. Most of Iran's buildings are designed to include

Lofti
The mausoleum, or burial place, of Shah Nematollah Vali is an excellent example of Islamic architecture. It is located in the town of Mahan.

Islamic features, such as domes, courtyards, and **minarets**. Buildings are often decorated with white plasterwork, colorful tile designs, and intricate mosaics.

Leisure

Iranians are sociable people, so they especially enjoy activities that include their families and friends. Other than visits and get-togethers, rural Iranians have very few leisure activities available to them. City dwellers, however, can choose from a variety of activities.

In summer, the weather is so hot that most shops and offices close in the afternoon. People often sleep after

Left: Iranians in urban areas enjoy riding bicycles and relaxing in the park. During summer, children can play in the parks until after midnight.

Left: Mountain resorts in Iran are popular places for skiing and relaxing. Some peaks in the northern part of the country are snowcapped all year long.

eating lunch. In the evening, when the air is cooler, people like to walk, shop, and eat at restaurants. Many cities have amusement parks that stay open late on summer nights.

In winter, skiing is a popular activity for people living in cities close to the mountains. People from Tehran, for example, ski every Friday on slopes in the Elburz Mountains.

Sports

Unofficially, soccer is Iran's national sport. All cities have soccer teams, and Tehran has ten soccer stadiums. One of them can seat up to 100,000 fans.

Volleyball, table tennis, martial arts, shooting, and horseback riding are also popular sports in Iran. Iranians enjoy wrestling, too. Wrestling events are held in gymnasiums called *zurkhaneh* (ZOOR-kah-nah), which means "house of strength."

Above: Iran's national soccer team played well in the 1998 World Cup championship held in France. Iran won in the first round against the United States but then lost to Germany.

Women and Sports

For most sports events in Iran, men and women are separated. Men can attend soccer matches anywhere in the country. Only recently, however, have women been allowed to attend matches in major cities. Unless women follow strict Islamic rules about clothing, they may perform sports in women-only stadiums.

Below:
Iranian women are excellent at show jumping and other horseback riding events. Islamic laws, however, make careers in sports difficult for Muslim women to pursue.

Festivals

The Iranian New Year, called *Noruz* (no-ROOZ), has been celebrated for thousands of years. It is Iran's biggest festival, starting on the first day of spring and lasting up to two weeks.

For one month each year, Muslims celebrate *Ramazan* (RAHM-ah-zahn), or Ramadan, which is a time of fasting. All healthy adults must not eat, drink, or smoke during daylight hours. At the end of Ramazan, they enjoy a feast known as *Eid-e Fetr* (EED-eh FET-reh).

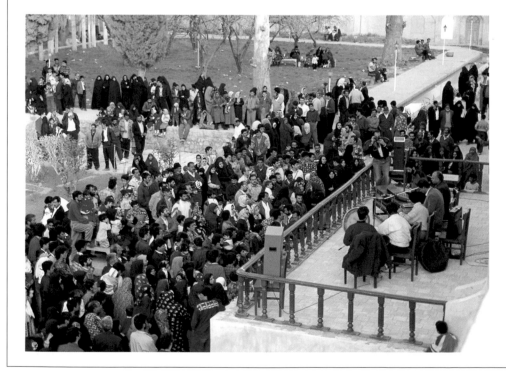

Left: Residents of Mahan hold an outdoor concert to celebrate the thirteenth day of Noruz, the Iranian New Year.

Muslims celebrate *Eid-e Qorban* (EED-eh GHOR-bahn), or the Feast of the Sacrifice, approximately two months after Ramazan. At this time, many Muslims make a **pilgrimage** to Mecca in Saudi Arabia. Shi'ite Muslims also celebrate the birthdays of their saints.

The Iranian government allows non-Muslim religious groups to celebrate their own holidays. Easter is an important festival for Iran's Christian people.

Food

Some Iranian foods are commonly found in other Middle Eastern countries, but many Iranian dishes are unique. Meals usually consist of rice, served with meat, and vegetable stews that combine sweet and sour flavors. Soups, kebabs, and omelettes are also popular in Iran. Iranian cooking uses a lot of green herbs, dried fruits and nuts, and fruit pastes.

Below: Iran has a variety of breads, all of which are baked in clay ovens. Fresh, hot bread is available several times each day.

Left: Iranian foods are served on large platters. The diners choose exactly what and how much they want. The dishes are placed on a tablecloth that is spread out on a carpet. Diners sit on the carpet around the tablecloth to eat.

Many Iranians follow food rules that define all foods as either "hot" or "cold," based on how a food affects the person eating it. Hot foods include sweets and meats. Cold foods include yogurt and fish.

Sweets and Snacks

Iranians enjoy rice puddings and pastries, especially baklava, which has layers of crisp, paper-thin pastry dough filled with nuts and coated with sugar syrup. Favorite snacks include dried fruits and nuts.

A B C

TURKEY

ARMENIA

AZERBAIJAN

CASPIAN

SEA

TURKMENISTAN

1

WEST
AZERBAIJAN

ARDABIL

EAST
AZERBAIJAN

GILAN

GOLESTAN

ZANJAN

KORDESTAN

QAZVIN

ELBURZ

MAZANDARAN

M O U N T A I N S

IRAQ

TEHRAN

■ Mount Damavand
(18,606 ft / 5,671 m)

SEMNAN

KERMANSHAHAN

HAMADAN

TEHRAN

KHORASAN

QOM

MARKAZI

2

ILAM

LORESTAN

ESFAHAN

CHAHAR
MAHALL VA
BAKHTIARI

Kalun River

ZAGROS

• Esfahan

YAZD

KHUZESTAN

KOHKILUYEH VA
BOYER AHMADI-YE
SARDIR

Pasargadae

• Mahan

Persepolis

KUWAIT

Shiraz

• Bam

3

SAUDI ARABIA

BUSHEHR

FARS

KERMAN

Persian

HORMOZGAN

BAHRAIN

Gulf

Gulf of Oman

QATAR

────── State Boundary

────── Provincial Boundary

■ Capital

● City

～～ River

4

UNITED ARAB
EMIRATES

OMAN

D

IRAN

N

AFGHANISTAN

PAKISTAN

SISTAN VA
BALUCHESTAN

Tropic of Cancer

Afghanistan D2–D3
Ardabil B1
Armenia A1
Azerbaijan A1–B1

Bahrain B4
Bam C3
Bushehr B3

Caspian Sea B1
Chahar Mahall va
   Bakhtiari B2

East Azerbaijan
   A1–B1
Elburz Mountains
   B1–B2
Esfahan (clty) B2
Esfahan (province)
   C2–B3

Fars B3–C3

Gilan B1
Golestan C1
Gulf of Oman C4

Hamadan B2
Hormozgan
   C3–C4

Ilam A2
Iraq A1–A3

Karun River B2–B3
Kerman C3–C4
Kermanshahan A2
Khorasan C1–D3
Khuzestan B2–B3
Kohkiluyeh va
   Boyer Ahmadl-ye
   Sardir B3
Kordestan A1–B2
Kuwait A3

Lorestan A2–B2

Mahan C3
Markazi B2
Markazi Mountains
   A1–D4
Mazandaran B1–B2
Mount Damavand
   B2

Oman C4

Pakistan D3–D4
Pasargadae B3
Persepolis B3
Persian Gulf B3–B4

Qatar B4
Qazvin B1–B2
Qom B2

Saudi Arabia A3–B4
Semnan B2–C2
Shiraz B3
Sistan va
   Baluchestan
   C3–D4

Tehran (city) B2
Tehran (province)
   B2
Turkey A1
Turkmenistan
   C1–D2

United Arab
   Emirates B4–C4

West Azerbaijan A1

Yazd C2–B3

Zagros Mountains
   B2–B3
Zanjan B1–B2

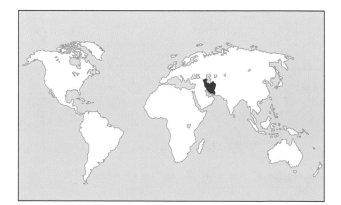

Quick Facts

Official Name	The Islamic Republic of Iran
Capital	Tehran
Official Language	Persian, or Farsi
Population	65,619,636 (2000 estimate)
Land Area	636,296 square miles (1,648,000 square km)
Provinces	Ardabil, Bushehr, Chahar Mahall va Bakhtiari, East Azerbaijan, Esfahan, Fars, Gilan, Golestan, Hamadan, Hormozgan, Ilam, Kerman, Kermanshahan, Khorasan, Khuzestan, Kohkiluyeh va Boyer Ahmadi-ye Sardir, Kordestan, Lorestan, Markazi, Mazandaran, Qazvin, Qom, Semnan, Sistan va Baluchestan, Tehran, West Azerbaijan, Yazd, Zanjan
Highest Point	Mount Damavand 18,606 feet (5,671 m)
Major River	Karun River
Major Mountains	Elburz range, Markazi range, Zagros range
Main Religion	Islam
Major Festivals	Ashura, Eid-e Fetr, Eid-e Qorban, Noruz
Currency	Rial (1,747.50 IRR = U.S. $1 as of 2000)

Opposite: The Gate of All Nations is located in Persepolis.

44

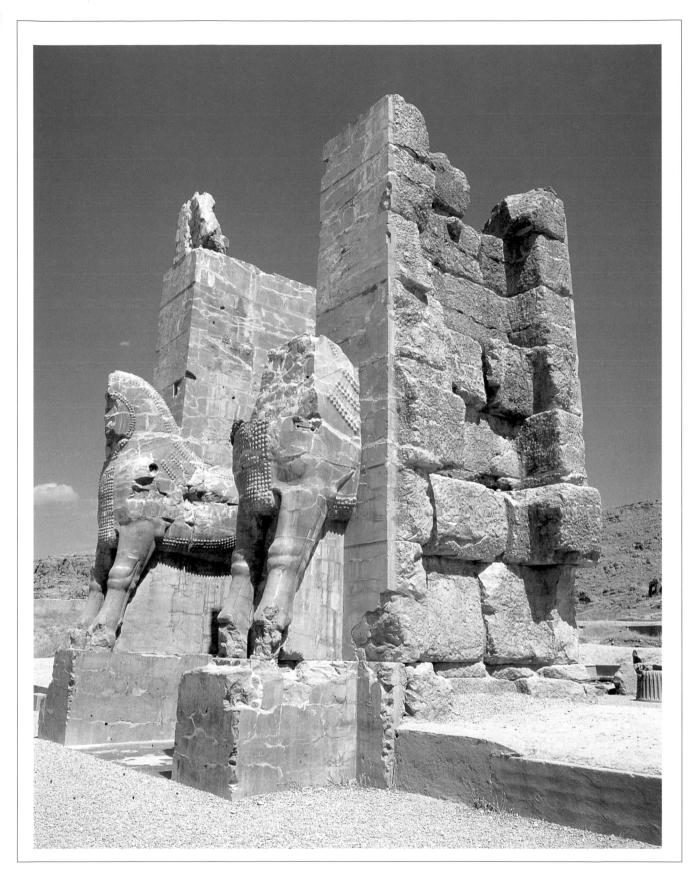

Glossary

archaeologists: scientists who study ancient peoples and their cultures.

artisans: skilled workers who create handmade crafts.

autocratic: having complete and unlimited power.

circulates: moves around or flows through from place to place.

coronation: the act of crowning a king, queen, or other ruler.

dynasty: a family of rulers who inherit their power.

elevation: the height, or altitude, of a place above sea level.

emblem: a figure, sign, or symbol that stands for an object or idea and is used to identify a person, group, or nation.

ethnic: related to a certain race or culture of people.

exile: the state of being sent away by force from a person's native land.

feudal: related to an ancient political system in which subjects pledged their service to a lord in exchange for protection and the use of land.

inscriptions: words that are painted, printed, or engraved on a hard surface, often as a dedication.

juries: groups of people selected to listen to the facts of court trials and make decisions based on law.

minarets: the tall thin towers attached to Muslim mosques, from which people are called to prayer.

nomadic: related to people who move from place to place within a region.

persecuted: treated cruelly and unfairly for reasons related to politics, race, or religion.

pilgrimage: a journey made to a sacred place as an act of religious devotion.

plateau: a large area of high, flat land that rises sharply above the land around it.

sanctions: measures taken by a country to restrict trade and official contact with another country that has broken international law.

seminary: an institution of higher learning that trains its students to be ministers of a religious faith.

sovereign: of the highest rank or power.

subtropical: nearby or bordering the hot, damp areas closest to the equator.

Zoroastrians: members of a Persian religion started by the prophet Zoroaster in the sixth century B.C.

More Books to Read

Alexander the Great. What's Their Story? series. Andrew Langley (Oxford University Press Children's Books)

Forty Fortunes: A Tale of Iran. Aaron Shepard (Clarion Books)

Iran. Enchantment of the World series. Mary Virginia Fox (Children's Press)

Iran: Land of the Peacock Throne. Exploring Cultures of the World series. William Spencer (Benchmark Books)

Islamic Festivals. Celebrate series. Khadijah Knight (Heinemann Library)

Kurds. Endangered Cultures series. Ann Carey Sabbah (Smart Apple Media)

Muslim Mosque. Places of Worship series. Angela Wood (Gareth Stevens)

The Persian Empire: Cultures of the Past series. Karen Zeinert (Benchmark Books)

Videos

Iran and Iraq. (A & E Home Video)

Islam: A Closer Look. (Tapeworm)

Ramadan. (Library Video)

Travel the World by Train: Near & Middle East. (Pioneer Entertainment)

Web Sites

www.arabiannights.org/rubaiyat/

www.intercaspian.com

www.jamaat.org/islam/Muhammad.html

www.lexicorient.com/e.o/iran.htm

Due to the dynamic nature of the Internet, some web sites stay current longer than others. To find additional web sites, use a reliable search engine with one or more of the following keywords to help you locate information about Iran. Keywords: *Cyrus the Great, Islam, Kurds, Noruz, Persian empire, Qur'an, Tehran.*

Index